PEOPLE, HORSES, AND ME!

A PERSONAL INSIGHT
INTO WHY I LOVE WHAT I DO

Julie Gould

People, Horses, and Me!

By Julie Gould

This book was first published in Great Britain in paperback during March 2022.

ISBN: 979-8428523355

This book is written in memory of Mark Stanley Smoothy 04/06/1962 – 16/01/2015.

A truly unique person who is missed by all, taken far too young.

Thank you to the Smoothy family for allowing me to manage my Julie Gould livery services on your amazing farm, for all your support over the last 31 years.

The following events, people and horses have been the reason I love my job so much, and long may it continue.

Happy reading to each and every one of you.

Laugh, love and be happy.

Julie Gould

Contents

About The Author

A passionate horse woman, the author describes herself as "half horse, half human". The very definition of the word "equine".

She was born in Harold Hill Essex, one of seven children. From an early age she loved horses and used to watch a 1970s children's TV programme called Follyfoot which was probably where the horse addiction started.

Her first horse ride was at 10 years of age, and she never looked back. After leaving school a career involving horse was inevitable. And it was working at a riding school where she met her husband, Rob.

She went on to gain her teaching qualifications whilst raising a family and starting a livery business. In the meantime, carrying on freelance teaching, pony club teaching, lecturing at Writtle college to achieve more qualifications and experience. Among her equine qualifications, she is a level 3 accredited professional coach registered with the British Horse Society.

Her 45 year horse addiction has been epic, lots of trials and tribulations with many stories to tell. This book is only the tip of the iceberg, with lots of fun joy and laughter and meeting the most amazing people along the way.

Her poor family and friends have suffered neglect because of her horsey addiction for which she apologises to them from the bottom of her heart. But she couldn't, wouldn't change a thing.

Julie thanks you all so much for sticking with her as friends and family. She truly loves you all.

How it All Started

I came to Home Farm, it was wet cold and dark I was greeted and shown round be a fella called Mark. He was tall and quite sturdy with oodles of charm he told me all the history of Pyrgo Palace Home Farm.

It had a lovely feel but needed extensive repair, but I got the feeling he really did care.

I moved in and settled, made the horses a bed. That was the day I met Mark's father Fred.

Fred was the boss it was very clear to see he came round the yard to introduce himself to me.

The rules were explained there will be no bending, if you over step the mark there will be an unhappy ending.

With total respect and full understanding, I followed the rules with the yard slowly expanding.

Mark asked me nicely if I would like to do the works, he said it was hard but with plenty of perks.

We started off slowly as the business grew but we have always been honest loyal and true.

The yard at Home Farm is great place to be it has always been a place that's been very good to me. The riding is good and the facilities amazing, and as for the horses there is plenty of grazing.

Respect on the yard is a very big thing be courteous respectful and no bad cursing.

You would have to go further for your horse to be happy, we once even cured a horse that was nappy.

We will cater for any horse good or bad but we will not be joyed with an owner being sad. The people and horses that come to Home Farm will be treated fairly and come to no harm.

The entrance to Home Farm

Fred and Mark

Fred and Mark what more can I say, it was a very special day when they came my way. They were a pair who cared and demanded respect any skulduggery they could easily detect.

It was their farm and that was made clear, if you break any rules please run in fear. Like it or lump it you will do as we say are you happy with that? The answer was okay.

I love that attitude, it was hard at the start but loving Home Farm was always in my heart.

The Rules

Enter this yard and you will abide by the rules, if you break any of these you must be a fool enter quite slowly do not go at speed, there are animals and children this rule you must head.

Park in the car park don't block any gates, please park sensibly for the sake of your mates.

Proceed to the yard no shouting or screaming, people in the cottages may be sleeping and dreaming.

Be courteous polite get on with your jobs, muck out your horses, your thoroughbred and cobs.

Keep the yard clean fork up all your muck, be sure to throw it up with a very high chuck, pick all your muck up when you use the arena. If you don't pick it up the camera will have seen you.

Its for everyone's safety the rules we obey, especially if you like the yard and do wish to stay.

No dogs allowed and keep your kids in line, you will find this info on a warning sign. No smoking allowed take all rubbish home with you.

The dustbins are full and this has been an issue, if you are unsure please ask for advice. We really do want to keep our lovely yard nice.

It's safe, clean and tidy and of that we are proud, please come on your own as we don't like a crowd.

If these rules are followed by one and all, the emergency services will not get a call. Safety is upmost we all need to stay well, if you need to know more please give me a bell.

My phone is always on please give it a go, the number to call ends in 060.

Aeroplane Crash

It was early September to be precise the sixth, when I wish in the morning I had my Weetabix. It started in the morning taking the horses to the field, when they got spooked and I nearly got killed.

That dog in the bushes scared the horses the SOD, the horses took off and all over me they trod. Off to the hospital bruised black and blue we were lucky, straight in there wasn't a queue.

Not too sad only bruised with a broken nose, but it's all part of the job and that's how it goes. Back to the yard in pain and feeling poor, you would have thought that was enough but then there was more.

Jan was out riding, she went up to the top. When out of the sky a light aeroplane did drop.

On to the field flipping on to its back, crash bang wallop and a great big crack. Jan came back she beat the speed of sound to get some help if anyone was around.

Off we went to the site of the plane, to see if the pilot had suffered any pain. He was covered in blood and had a few minor cuts. I had to admire his courage and guts, I took of my triangular I had been wearing it all day.

I could see he was nervous, but he didn't like to say, I am going to make you feel better if I put this on your head. He didn't like the colour it was yellow brown and red.

It had seen some action whilst working on the yard, but using it to dress his wound was deffo on the cards. Little did we know he had been up to no good, he was dropping off drugs wherever he could.

It was a hell of a day and I am glad it came to an end, all was okay it took a few weeks to mend.

No damage done and no lasting harm, it was all in a day's work at the yard Home Farm.

Julies Angels

My beautiful peaches Courtney, Rachel and Gem. What would I do if I didn't have them?

Gem so quiet caring but tough, Courtney lovely but feisty and rough.

Rachel well let's see what can I say, Rach will be Rachel and she will do it her way.

I love all of these peaches with all of my heart, as they have been with me right from the start.

They came to the yard and I helped with their riding, so when I needed help there was going to be no hiding.

They each started working at weekends to start, but they loved the work and I knew we would never part. They really work hard and will do anything, if am in need I just give them a ring.

They are like family to me without a doubt, I can rely on these peaches they don't mess me about.

These girls need to know how much they are respected, as working for me they will never be rejected.

Rachel noisy, bolshy, and strong. Gem the peach who could never do wrong. Courtney so tough, resilient a star she always gets on with it she will go far.

My life would be nothing without their hard work they have been loyal to me, an amazing perk.

So rest assured peaches you have been amazing to Julie, that's why she loves you honest, deeply and truly.

So long may our friendship blossom and stick, and I'll see you on Monday for our massive poo pick.

Naked Man on The Perimeter

I love these spring mornings, fresh bright and breezy. There's lots of turning out to do it will never be easy.

It was on one of these mornings quite fresh and cold, when I came across a naked man walking strong and bold. He was walking on the perimeter with his backpack on his back, when I looked over briefly and I could see his back, sack and crack!

I was quite shocked and stunned not a sight I had seen before, a thought crossed my mind – I hope there ain't no more.

I rush down to the farm to report to Fred and Mark, they took off in the Land rover to the part of the farm called "park".

He was running across the fields and jumped into a great big ditch, he was wearing no clothes not one single stitch. They asked him, "What you up too?"

He said, "I am just walking free", they explained to him politely that this is not the place to be.

There are special places to go if you are walking in the nude but not on public footpaths as it is classed as very rude.

He dressed himself quite fast, the police were called to talk. They told the man that in this area you need clothes on to walk.

So with a verbal warning and the rules of naked walking, the man was let on his way with no further talking.

The Farriers

They come to the yard there are lots, quite a few, the intentions of them are your horses to shoe.

Over the years we have seen many, young and old. They are one of a kind very strong, tough and bold.

Don, Sid and Lloyd to name but a few. If you want your horse shod the please join the queue.

One thing's a must when the farriers arrive, you make them some tea that's what makes them thrive.

Full set? pair of fronts? Or just a simple trim, please make it clear what your horse needs of him.

To encourage him back he also likes a cake, make sure it's his favourite for your horse's sake. Thank you to all the farriers that have been to the yard. Your services are invaluable to keep our horse's hooves hard.

Long may it continue your services to us, make sure you are on time and then we won't cuss. NO FOOT, NO HORSE is the fact that we know. So keep shoeing horses for your knowledge to grow.

Lloyd Vant

Lloyd our farrier is leaving us he has a better job, it will be so much easier and plus he will earn a few more bob.

He has done it long enough picking up all of those hoofs, he is gonna find it easier cleaning all those roofs. He is the best farrier any horse could need, it is such a shame he was just getting up to speed.

We really will miss you Lloyd you are a total ledge! But obviously we respect the fact you need the extra wedge.

Thank you, Lloyd, for all you have done, we have put you too the test. We wish you well from all of us you really are the best!

You know by the way, you cannot get away Julie will not let you go. My dolly really needs you since she has got that seedy toe. We wish you well in all you do, you will never be forgot. We are very happy with your mate he has filled a great big slot.

The Vets

Where would we be without our lovely vets, always there for us looking after our precious pets.

Chris, Jane, Eric and Anna to name but a few. If you need any help they will come to the yard for you.

Lameness? Colic? Abscess? no matter what the prob they will come along to see you and do a proper job.

Reliable, keen, professional and very polite. They really do love their job as long as your horse doesn't bite.

They have been there for us for years, there is a great big team. They run the practise with such ease, well that is how it would seem.

Thank you all for all of your care, you really are so swell, there really is no better vet if your animal is not well. Long may it continue the care you always give, we want our pets to be healthy and longer they will live.

Vet Nurse

Olivia Proverbs-Grover a lovely caring nurse, I am hoping that you are going to like this perfect little verse.

It will sum you up in a very short space of time, knowing you for many years has been totally sublime.

Beautiful stunning a total joy to know, you are so very clever. Your vet nurse career will grow, well done to you for passing your veterinary nurse test. You have studied really hard you really are the best.

Good luck to you in the future in everything you do, to employ you as a vet nurse there will be a very long queue.

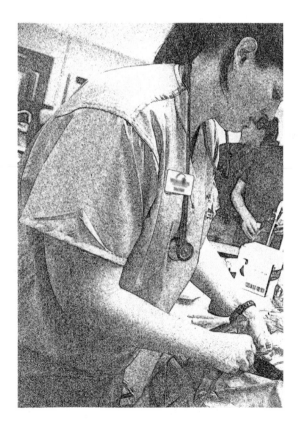

Jess

Wow what a horse woman! That jess she is a star, she is professional, kind and firm she really will go far.

She understands the horses better than anyone I know, where others cry off jess will give it a go.

No short cuts, no gadgets and no bits that are too strong. This is the problem and where it all goes wrong. The methods that she uses is give it some more time, then they will always come right when they reach their prime.

Patience, understanding get to the route of the prob. Ride your horse daily he was born to do the job.

Build up a bond, get to know your horse well. I know they can't talk but body language will tell. Look for the signs if your horse is in any pain, if you do miss these signs no progress you will gain.

Trust patience and tack that does fit, turn out your horse well with good quality kit. Teeth, back and hooves will be done when due. Then you will have a happy horse and also happy you.

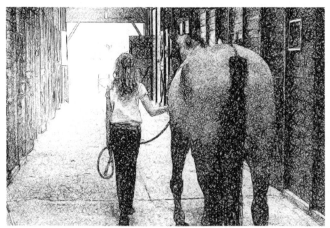

Take your horse out when all these things are done, then collect all of your winnings that you will have won.

Jayde

I was once called up by a lady called pearl, she said to me "Julie would you have a job for my girl?" I replied to her, I might have please call me next week.

She sounded so happy, so lovely and so meek. The girl in question was the delightful Jayde, she came during the holidays she helped and then she stayed.

I liked her a lot, very honest and kind. And that is a quality I really don't mind. I gave her a start and this is the date, I waited that day and she was two hours late.

I was worried sick, my heart was in my mouth. She said when she came the bus went north instead of south. That started a friendship one I will never forget, Jayde is one of the kindest and nicest people I have ever met. I asked her one day "Please take the cobs to grass". She forgot to do it, she was sitting on her arse. I took them myself and said, "Jayde you forgot!" she said I am so sorry Julie but I do love you a lot!

Well what could I say, I was stunned and couldn't speak. I laughed my head off and thought how lovely such cheek! Jayde is so special and one of a kind, the sort of person so very hard to find.

I am so lucky to have her in my life, she has since got married and is now Steve's wife, she is still at the yard and looks after Skye. Her standards of care are very high!

She grooms her and walks her, lays her a great big bed. Gives her carrots apples and short feed when she is fed.

Long may it continue our friendship is strong, in my life our Jayde could do no wrong. Thank you, Jayde, for you have worked very hard, long may it continue our friendship at Home Farm yard.

Jane and Hannah

Jane and Hannah are a mother daughter team, knowing these girls is a total dream. Fun, loving and polite they are total joys. They each have a horse they are both boys, hansel and boxer are two very well schooled horses.

They have their lessons weekly one of my life long courses, we jump we run we nearly get control we are working on the boys to try and lower the poll. We never give up it has been a long session, but over all I have seen the progression.

Thanks to the ladies we always have a blast, please can you make sure you don't canter too fast. I know I keep on repeating about the scales of training, but you will never achieve your goals if you don't ride when raining. Come on girls we will get there one day these two beauties really are okay.

Heels down legs long sit up tall let's do a dressage test, I really can't wait to go out you are really simply the best. Brook farm is calling let's make a date, we will be very early we won't be late.

I feel we are ready come on let's give it a try, if it doesn't go as planned we will drink wine and cry!

Maybel.

Maybel a horse so lovely and kind, a table top back and a whopping behind. She once ate some apples the bag and all! It was three days past until natures call. She was one in a million just like her mum her heart was huge but not as big as her bum.

She had a great life she was loved until the end memories of Maybel will never descend, a place in my heart and memories will always be there for the lovely Maybel a big beautiful honest mare.

Ebony Jane

Ebony jane a beautiful black mare very, very broad with lots of hair, black and hairy a sturdy cob a lively ride but not a dob. A very strong girl with a lively mind no doubt about it one of a kind, a stunning horse strong and keen cross her path and she could be mean.

Leading her about you needed the bridle if you use just the headcollar it was suicidal, looked after and cared for by the lovely Jan to make Ebbo's life better she did all that she can.

Life for us all sadly has to come to an end, especially with old age and things you can't mend, so over the bridge to see all of your mates they will all be waiting at those pearly gates. You will always live on as one of the best, as over the years you put us all to the test.

Rest in peace you beautiful soul I will remember you always as my heart you stole.

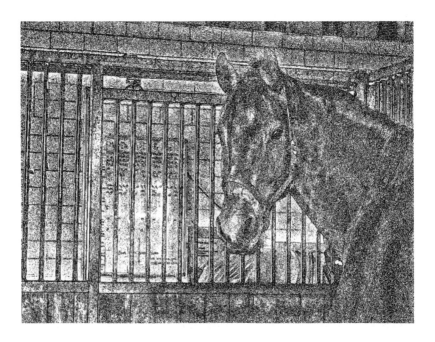

Indie

Kind, gorgeous and manners a total joy, Indie Dekeyser a beautiful chestnut boy. He was treated by Lin and Colin like a royal king, he never wanted for one single thing.

What a life he had with us at Home Farm with his perfect impressive good looks and charm, memories of Indie will live on forever, our thoughts of you will never sever.

Much love and hugs from us all to you pair, don't be strangers we really do care.

Duke

Duke a legend a big excitable bay, if he were human he would actually be gay. Kind, stressy and sassy he really had the lot.

You could be walking along quietly, and he would suddenly loose the plot, joggy, short striding and back behind the bit "oh stop it Duke you're acting like a tit".

Karen did well to ride that boy I don't really think she had much joy, however so kind with a gay little wicker one thing is for sure he wasn't a kicker.

Duke lived a long life he was bold until the end, it comes to us all with things you can't mend but you will live on as one of the best. It's time to move on for the ultimate rest, there will be lots of friends waiting all of your mates! Over that rainbow bridge to the pearly gates.

So long farewell your life was so brill, you certainly will have big hooves too fill. Who will fill them I am not really sure, but one thing is for certain there will be more.

Marley

The earth started moving the lorry was shaking, the ramp opened up and there stood Marley the earth was quaking.

Big bold and strong a very handsome beast! Get me to the stable for that hay and short feed feast. I think he will like it here at the yard Home Farm. He pulls lots of faces but he will do you no harm.

Horses stay clear this stable is my place, if you do I will squeal out, kick the wall and pull a face. I have warned you I made it clear that my attitude is ripe and my only defence is to attack the drainpipe!

I will settle down but all in my time so please be patient I have committed no crime, I am not very good when being handled in the stable but get on my back and I will show you I am able.

I love to be ridden I walk fast and soldier on, I can even out walk the handsome regal Ron.

Come on you horses who hack out on my ride, trot on a bit and get up by my side. When out in the field I am guarding the gate. I am keen to get in but I will just have to wait, please hurry Karen I am waiting for my feed a big boy like me is in desperate need.

Feed me groom me and treat me like a lord, and I will be the best horse anyone can afford.

The Arabs

It was a lovely find day in the middle of May, when the Arabs arrived and made my day. Polly and Melody two gorgeous mares looking at these two answered all my prayers. Carla and Vanessa adored these two dolls so they decided to breed and get two lovely foals.

Leo came first a very special boy working with him is a total joy, he is frightened of totally everything on earth and when you tack up don't mention the girth.

He loves to run and gallop really fast working with him has been a total blast. Then came Thea so elegant and right, don't go in the stable! she may kick or bite, she loves her stable! it's the best thing in life enter at your peril her temperament is rife!

The four of these beauties have been a joy to know, Thea will be a winner when she goes to a show. Long may it continue this bond that we share, we hope that at Home Farm you will always be there.

Tracey

Tracey the girl I respect very much, she is so high up on a Pedestal you could not touch. She comes to the yard and rides Jackie's Feline, the bruises she has are quite obscene. She loves that feline but I do not know why, she kicks her and bites her and even makes her cry.

But what I love best she is so caring and dear, she goes down to the fields and keeps the poo clear. Tracey my darling we all love you so much please keep poo picking you have the golden touch.

Abbey

Its Abbeys birthday she is turning 21! Let life begin with lots and lots of fun, it's a shame it's in lockdown how very, very sad, as long as we all stay healthy it won't be that bad.

It will be a good time to ride and enjoy your lovely boy, we will soon be back in the rat race, no time no fun and no joy.

Enjoy your life you are 21, you now have the key to the door we wish you all the best and much, much more!

Having fun is a must it's definitely not a crime, make the most of all of your life and please don't waste any time.

Angie

Poor Angie our lovely, sweet girl, Friday last week did not go very well
it started really lovely the weather really bright. But in the afternoon
Angie gave us all a fright, she wandered into the yard dazed and in a
blur.

We said "what has happened?" she replied she really isn't sure. Angie
could not remember but she had blood all over her face. We had to call
an ambulance she was not in a good place, they took her in the
ambulance and cared for her really well.

But her memory was lost, and we don't know how she fell, her
cheekbone was broken and her face badly cut. There was lots of blood
and mud and on her shoulder, and her butt.

It is still a big mystery what happened on that day, but lucky all is well
now and our Angie is okay. She is a very tough girl she handles the
horses with care. She will soon be back up too see her moody mare.

Grace has really missed her but she has enjoyed the rest, we are looking
forward to seeing Angie she really is the best.

Shirley and Steve

Steve and Shirley, what a lovely pair! Such honest and caring people they really do care! Helpful and hardworking a credit to the yard, they really are trojans they work so very hard.

I have known them both for years it's been a total pleasure, my lovely friendship with you I respect and always treasure. Much love to you both you are always in my mind, what stands out so much you are both very kind.

41 years married what an amazing goal, Steve Shirley said could you get her another foal.

Rachel and Alice

Rachel and Alice a match made in heaven! I have known Rachel since she was aged seven. The nicest person you would ever wish to meet, funny adorable the whole package complete! She has pushed me to the limit I will have to admit, but how can you not love her she is an adorable git!

Alice, I haven't known well for very long but what does shine through is that she is very strong, I am wishing you both all the very best as being a married couple will put you to the test.

Always remember these very words I say, get this in order – work, rest and play.

Marriage is forever through lots of trouble and strife, be tolerant patient and honest throughout your married life.

Wish you both love, health and happiness to you two. I cannot wait to see you at the wedding venue.

Much love and hugs too you two beautiful souls, I am hoping that you always achieve your future goals!

Debbie

Debbie is a friend of mine, she is an equineaholic! It's all she loves to do all day is horse and pony folic.

Horses, horses, horses - we have a one track mind, it's in our blood a way of life we are just two of a kind. We love to smell that scent of horse it gives up satisfaction, to care for them as we do is just an addictive attraction.

Mucking out and filling nets that's how we fill our day, I tell you now with me and deb we won't have it any other way. We love it to eternity this horse muck life we lead it keeps us out of trouble and gives us all we need.

Long may it continue it keeps us young and fit, so horses keep it coming so we can shovel loads more shit!

George (Jenny)

It is with great affection I will remember you, standing by the muck hill quietly admiring the view. Reciting all of the riddles that you really love to tell, when you came down to Home Farm yard too see your lovely girl. It was always such a pleasure to chat to you and kay, when you both came to the yard it really made my day.

I was really very sad when Kaz told me you were not well, I was very upset I will miss those rhymes you would tell. You passed away soon after an even sadder time, life can be so cruel death such a crime.

Memories are treasured my thoughts are with all of you, please call me if there is anything at all I can do.

Jenny and Tia

Jenny and Tia two beautiful girls, if they were jewels, they would be the best pure pearls! Honest, true, kind caring and calm they will help you out do you no harm.

Tia can be ridden by young or old she is very, very quiet but steps out big and bold, Jenny is around to help out whenever she can I am currently trying to find her a kind and caring man.

Its Jenny's birthday today and she really needs to know, we are all here for her to make her blossom and grow.

So happy birthday gorgeous you really are a gem! So trust me and believe me this yard needs more of them. Have a great day Jenny we all wish you well, and if you need anything at all just give me a bell.

Livvy and Kitty

Livvy and Kitty, a perfect pair, a lovely horse a sturdy bay mare. Lovely natured quiet and calm perfect for walking and trotting around the farm. The fun has just started there is a long way to go, but once they have bonded their confidence will grow.

Riding and caring for kitty will definitely be fun they will learn to trot and canter eventually to run. I am so glad for Livvy the mare is so right, she has got a lovely nature she doesn't kick or bite!

Happiness always much riding you will do, to find a lovely horse like this there will be a very long queue.

Scarlet and Lacey

Scarlett was riding lacey in the school, they together were looking really cool then lacey started to leap and jump Scarlett flew off with a great big bump.

Scarlett jumped up in quite a panic she had never actually been so fast and manic, she got back on and all was well we said to Lacey, "You naughty girl". She will ride again she won't be scared but on next week's lesson we will be well prepared.

Rocky and Junior

Rocky and Junior wow what a pair, as long as they were together, they didn't have a care. Sadly departed Junior's life must go on, even if Junior thought where has Rocky gone?

We will never forget Rocky that kind and lovely boy, his manners perfect he was a total joy. The life of a lord he had for sure, that lovely boy could not have wanted for more.

No more suffering and no more pain, rest in peace Rocky until we meet again.

Junior

My name is Junior and I have a story to tell of when I met the Taylors and in gods pocket I fell, they have loved me and fed me as if I were a king I have never ever wanted for one single thing.

However over the years I have not played ball they expected me to come when my name they would call, I wanted to come but I loved all the grass to be perfectly honest I have been a proper arse.

I did try to tell them but I could not talk, if you wanna go riding you will just have to walk. I am not coming in my field is my life and don't send that Julie her language is rife.

I just want you to know I have really had the best, I am tired and not feeling good I really need the rest. I am crossing the bridge to see Rocky my best friend one hell of an era has come to an end.

Me and Rocky reunited at last that life you have me was one hell of a blast. Thank you so much from the bottom of my heart it is so sad but we do have to part the memories of us will always live on. We won't be forgotten although we are gone.

Bye bye for now until we meet again, we will always be with you down memory lane.

The Muckers

There have been many muckers over the years, they have helped me at the yard facing all of their fears.

Mucking out turning out feeding and rugs! I owe them a lot of big kisses and hugs without all these muckers the job would not get done but whilst we are working we do have great fun.

We have tea and toast biscuits galore! and in Julie's box there are lots, lots more.

Laughing and joking whilst working away, Monday to Sunday we work every day.

It is hard work, cold, muddy and smelly. Please remember in the winter you need a good welly!

Thank you so much the risks are quite high, keep your wits about you or you will get a kick in the thigh.

Bitten crushed and trodden on toes it's all part of the job and that's how it goes. We must trudge on your feet will be sore but there is still lots to do and much, much more.

Long may it continue our mucking out fest, all of my muckers have been simply the best!

Maintenance Man

Where would we be without our maintenance man keeping the yard safe wherever he can, fences down? Burst pipes? Broken wall? Whatever the problem you can give him a call!

There is no limit to what he can do he will come round the yard and fix it for you, delivering the feeds and supplies to your horse he has extensive skills it's all part of the course.

I see him sometimes praying and wishing that the weekend would come and he could go fishing.

But that cannot be the work will not end there will always be something on the yard to mend, thank you so much for all that you do. The yard would be broken if it wasn't for you.

Pyrgo Shoot Boys

They come to the farm this is where they all meet, the centre of base is a shack called retreat.

It's in a quiet corner hidden away, its where del, bob and the boys spend most of the day.

Their intentions of coming are to look after the birds, they do talk a lot there are many, many words.

The pheasants are covered for water and feed if them boys could shoot well them birds would be dead!

But lucky for us the boys can't shoot very well, so all the birds live on and have a story to tell.

So good luck birds keep up with your hiding and you shall live on with no fear of subsiding.

The shoot must go on its all part of country life, but on the shoot days the noise is quite rife.

The noise is so loud the birds run and hide, the beaters cry out but the birds wont abide.

They are very cleaver them pheasants they know, that on shoot days out of cover don't go.

I am fond of these pheasants they do make me smile, they scurry around with plenty of style.

Long may it continue the shoot boys at the farm, it's all part of life it doesn't do any harm.

Harvey

Harvey a legend the pony of your dreams, he loves all the children well that is how it seems.

The children he has taught go on to ride well so they all love Harvey and have a story to tell.

Xenia, Jack and Amy to name but a few, if you want to ride Harvey, please join the queue.

We went to collect him from over in Kent, we saw him we loved him he seemed so content.

The lady who owned him said there is just one thing, when you try to catch him be patient and sing.

He will not be caught unless he wants to come in, that is so true it is his only sin.

He knows if you want him, he senses he can tell so the coming in phase does not go well.

The other little problem we noticed in time, is that having him shod is a total crime. He cried like a baby it made me so sad, he has to go barefoot but it isn't too bad.

We do love our Harvey he is still going strong, approaching 40 years and he can do no wrong.

A legend of a pony one of a kind, another like Harvey will be so hard to find.

Cookalicious

I can never forget the day I met cookie, a black and white cob young, calm and quite a rookie.

I went to collect him with Sandra and Stace, they were excited and happy I could see on their face.

We got to the yard where cookie was eating, there were children and guinea pigs it was a lovely greeting!

My thoughts of cookie were wow, he is a star.

To find another like this you would have to go far, the pony led out by a very young child. He was quiet and calm no sign of wild.

Straight up in the trailer no messing around, a million pound pony has just been found.

Since being at the yard he has been a winner, one thing is for sure he loves his dinner.

Cookie my boy you have landed on your feet, with your life at this yard you will have lots to eat.

Lucky young cookie you're a real family boy, the family you have really find you a joy.

Jackie and Courtney

Jackie and Courtney such great fun and loyal, if you didn't know better you would think they were royal.

No wimping no excuses let's give it a go, when you ask them a favour they never say no.

Friends like these are so truly dear, you don't let them wander you keep them so near.

Lazer, Meg and Feline had all the best, even thought they put the girls to the test.

They do like a challenge their horses are fast, they go round the perimeter and give them a blast. When we do lessons we do have some fun we work very hard the horses have to run.

My friendship with these two is honest and truly, even if bubba does get sick of hearing the word Julie.

Don't ever change girls you are two of a kind, and that is a special quality quite hard to find.

Thank you for all your help, love and care. My respect for you is high you're a very special pair.

Snappy Jess

A quirky little pony stunning looking to the eye, but for some unknown reason she knew how to make the kids cry.

Beautiful face with a long white mark, teeth very white and snappy like a shark.

She really made me laugh she was amazing fun, if she spotted a child she would chase them and run.

Gemma was leading her out of the stable one day, jess ran very fast gem was in her way. Gem fell on the floor she landed on her gut jess ran over her and kicked her up the butt!

Once you were riding her you really enjoyed the ride, but when on foot the kids would run and hide.

I never really understood the reason for her hate, but it was apparent she chased the children to the gate.

She will always hold a special place in my heart, giving her away was the heart breaking part.

There must have been a reason for the child kid phobia, it was all in the past before I got to know you no more riding no more pain. Just plenty of grass much weight you will gain.

Thank you for all of the things you taught me, one thing is for sure I never found your key.

Ebony's Haircut

Will you look after my beautiful bold mare, black and shiny with lovely long hair.

Of course I will that will be fine, no need to worry I will care for her as if she were mine. Whilst I was out riding two girls were helping me. I got back from riding they said come look and see!

We have tidied up Ebbo we have made her look good, they had cut her hair with scissors which they never should.

Oh my god I could not speak out, I wanted to say Noooo but I couldn't even shout, her beautiful black hair which had never been cut was lying on the floor behind the water butt.

I phoned up my friend I said she will need hair extensions, I don't care about the cost the price do not mention. The girl came along to replace the cut hair, it took all day, but I did not care.

She did not look nice her face was on show, and that was a sight we did not know.

Our poor Ebbo was missing her hair, as long as she was eating she didn't really care. The extensions went on they cost quite a lot but the girls paid up they didn't dare not!

All ended up well Ebbo was back hairy, it was an event that I dreaded as it was quite scary. The thought of this happening whilst in my care was a nightmare I do not wish to share.

All was resolved of that I am proud, the scissors were hidden no more cutting allowed.

Chukka

Chukka a mare beautiful and bay, if she were a human she would love to have her say. She knows what she wants she knows what she knows.

When she was competing she loved all the shows, she can't go in the field as she's very hard to catch. She also jumps the fences if she sees and lush grassy patch!

Her legs have been swollen her tendons are sore, she's feeling very sad quite low and poor.

But we all cheer her up she has days in the spa, she loves all the fuss she feels like a film star.

Kirsty, bob and Chris love her to bits they come and clean her out, and groom her with their kits. She loves a massage a deep tissue groom it makes her feel good, so she will blossom and bloom.

We love our Chuk she is one of a kind, the sort of horse so very hard to find mick might not think so he trims up her feet.

He will not give up will not accept defeat, she leans on him badly gives him a hard time. Anyone looking would think it's a crime.

Don't change chukka, we love you a lot but please behave yourself or we might lose the plot.

Mark Smoothy R.I.P

Funny, caring and would help in any way he could then his own health suffered and never should.

What would we do without him around the farm is dull without that laughing sound. Our hearts are sad I can see people moping, their faces drained but they are still coping.

Life goes on yes we know It will, the atmosphere is calm and very still. Mark, I heard you knew what we all thought of you, for hearts that are broken there is a very long queue.

Your memories and stories will live on forever, we will never forget you never, never, never.

We respect you we miss you what more can I say, we will see you in heaven but not sure what day.

Georgiana

Helpful, kind, caring, sensitive and lots more to say. When she does anything she does it her way. I first met her years ago she was only nine, I knew back then she would be totally divine.

She loved her guinea pigs she was so proud! She showed them off she loved a crowd.

Beautiful Georgiana a gorgeous peach, a pleasure to know a pleasure to teach.

Her boots were so big the ones she wore to the farm, she would have to wear callipers they did her no harm.

Her parents are lovely and support her so well, when the day of fruition comes there will be a story to tell.

What about the dog? they said no you can't keep, she kept him any way and the bills have been steep.

she's a strong minded girl but a heart of gold, she loves her grandad even though he is old.

Friends forever we will always be, there will never be another like the one and only she.

Livery Life Job

Where would we be without our livery life jobs, looking after thoroughbreds, Arabs and cobs.

Things that happen, treads kicks and bites. I have seen some things some terrible sights.

We walk through the field the feet are throbbing, no time to cry or time for sobbing.

Bruises backaches blisters and foot rot, most of these ailments we seem to have got.

It's all part of life when you look after horses, it's a great workout with life changing forces.

No time for illness no time for rest, doing this job puts your body to the test.

With your feet they get painful, sore and with bruises. But turning out horses gets done no excuses.

Plantar fasciitis and sciatica such pain, but just like the saying no pain no gain.

We still love our job we do honest truly, but in the back of my mind I think no foot no Julie.

So on we trudge no time to complain we struggle on and put up with the pain.

We love our job it's what we do, with the best of care, my work force crew.

Calendar Girls

Calendar girls what a great idea, raising money to buy arena gear. Sue idea she will take the pics just need to sort out the lovely chicks.

Who is up for the calendar date it will be fun, a good laugh it will be great!

Ladies that lunge will be the name, if will be popular and build our fame.

Black and white photos in the woods and the yard, taking the pics can't be that hard.

Keep your body covered with a little on show, lacey bits showing leaving Imagination to grow. So much fun we had that year, facing up to our exposure fear.

Karen, Julie, Kacey, Janine, Jill, Courtney, Sam and Jo, how much success we weren't to know. We sold so many we had to have more printed! By the end of the year we were truly minted.

We had enough money to buy some new jumps, so making the calendar did come up trumps.

Miss July

Gemma and Skye

What a lovely combo our Gemma and Skye, when she was younger she would jump very high.

She was quite a lively mare, a quirky spot. If you tried to catch her she would run off in trot.

When Gemma first got her she was funny with the tack, she would run around the stable if you put the saddle on her back.

She has been a good girl at cross country and jump. But for some reason lately travelling in the trailer has given her the hump, she will kick about and lean to the side so when she goes to a show to get there you ride.

Gemma has cared for her like she were a queen, but Skye hasn't been kind and sometime quite mean. Jade is her loaner she comes to muck out, you must be quiet you must shout.

Lately of years Skye has been lame, she has ring bone, so she is not quite the same. She can't be ridden some days she is quite sore but at 25 year old we could not want more.

Long may she live she has the life of a lord, she has all she needs and all that Gemma can afford.

Happiness always to Gem and Skye, my respect for you two is very high.

King

King a legend the horse of your dreams, if he were a cake he would have all of the cream! Teaching so many people to ride and love horses. Gaining respect from all of his sources.

The amount of people who love and respect this boy! He is out of this world he has been a total joy. Hacking, driving and jumping all heights all who have ridden him have never had any frights.

He would look after the riders and take good care, so at the end of the ride they were safe at the top and still there.

He had some dislikes! Bags and syringes if you went near him with these, he had nervous cringes.

Gemma and King have been together 20 years, facing all their horse riding good bits and fears. He came through some colic he wouldn't let go, so he lived to tell the tale for the veteran show.

Laila and King went to Brook Farm, they hacked there together it did them no harm. They did very well and got placed on the day, not bad for a 31 year old horse who did it his way.

Jimmie Houlder

They came to the yard Chris and Kelly looking for a stable, they were looking to buy a special horse it had to be willing and able.

16 foot mahogany and it has to be kind, I knew exactly what they meant it shouldn't be too hard to find.

Jimmy was found he came from afar, a fella called Clive he said he fits the bill and is easy to thrive. They ordered their stock 20 bales of woodchip, 10 bales of hay they thought that should be plenty to last for one day.

Kelly and Jim really did have a special bond until one day whilst out riding he threw her in the pond, he did not load that easy after a few bad trips.

Not to mention the haircut he didn't like the clips! I wrote her an ode one day many years ago to celebrate their relationship grow.

Ode to Jimmy Holder

There is a horse kept at Home Farm, he is handsome gorgeous and dull of charm I have known him now for many years.

And in that time he has grown big ears, Jimmy Holder is this horses name and within Home Farm he has grown with fame, he is the best he is full of trend if he were a person he would be my best friend.

25 years have now gone by and Jimmy is still around, he couldn't have found a better owner than the one he has found.

My First Liveries

My first ever liveries Jilly and Di they owned the tack shop they gave me a try, we managed the pony club and that's how we met. They will be friends I will never forget.

Abi and Brandy they're beautiful steeds, they performed well and suited all of their needs.

Abi a beautiful chestnut mare she was bread by David down at Abbotts dare, she was a thoroughbred mare lively but kind she loved her work she had an active mind. I took her to dressage we trained a lot, the first time out she totally lost the plot.

Very highly strung good looking quite stunning, we kept up the training and didn't stop running. Next few outings saw quite a good test, we got placed quite a lot she turned out the best.

Brandy a Welshy a strawberry boy, he was ridden by Roz she had lots of joy. Jilly was training to be a teacher of drama she lured me to her class to play Chief Weasel, such karma.

It was Toad's birthday from Toad of Toad Hall, it was so much fun we all had a ball, I told Jilly straight "Don't invite anyone from the yard" as to perform in front of them would be embarrassingly hard.

After months of training and lots of fun, toad from toad hall had a two night run, I was nervous quite frightened and had two glasses of wine but my lines I remembered I knew it would be fine.

I got there early was shaking like a leaf, when the curtain went up it was beyond belief. The whole of the audience was all from Home Farm I was shaking like a jelly far from calm.

I was Chief Weasel a funny role to play, I had to sing a song for toad on his birthday, the audience were laughing they made me laugh a lot.

I haven't lived it down, it was a cunning plot. These are the reasons that I love livery life forever. Memories live on forgotten never, ever, ever.

Daph

Daph was Fred's wife she stayed in all day, she answered the door when your livery you'd pay, she was always there she did the job well.

Daph always had a good story to tell, she loved her shoes she had 6 dozen pairs, they were her pride and joy fulfilled all her cares.

Daph had 2 donkeys she wanted something to do, Alvin and Barnaby were the original two. After their days came Sarah and Humpty, they were quite old and also quite dumpty.

Xenia arrived she was the first grandchild born, she came at the time when they'd harvest the corn. She came to Daph's and a few days she would stay, she'd come to the yard to ride Harvey and play.

It is with great pride I remember those days, they are often in my thoughts and that's where it stays.

The horse with beauty unsurpassed strength immeasurable grace unlike any other! still remains humble enough to carry a man on his back, I've often said there's nothing better for the inside of a man than the outside of the horse.

Megan Oswald

Printed in Great Britain
by Amazon

77978045R00037